Coleslaw

Recipes

© Copyright 2018. Laura Sommers.
All rights reserved.
No part of this book may be reproduced in any form or by any electronic or mechanical means without written permission of the author. All text, illustrations and design are the exclusive property of
Laura Sommers

Introduction 1

Classic Coleslaw 2

Blue Cheese Herb Coleslaw 3

Buffalo Coleslaw 4

Curry Coleslaw 5

Russian Coleslaw 6

Waldorf Coleslaw 7

Kohlrabi Apple Coleslaw 8

Grape Pecan Coleslaw 9

Barbecue Chicken Coleslaw 10

Cajun Coleslaw 11

Chipotle Coleslaw 12

Crispy Coleslaw 13

Carrot Pineapple Coleslaw 14

Kale Coleslaw 15

Light Coleslaw 16

Broccoli Ranch Coleslaw 17

Thai Coleslaw 18

Pepper Coleslaw 19

Hot Dressed Coleslaw 20

Apple Fennel Coleslaw 21

Creamy Coleslaw 22

Green Goddess Coleslaw 23

Korean Coleslaw 24

Caesar Coleslaw 25

Vinaigrette Coleslaw 26

Confetti Coleslaw 27

Herb Coleslaw 28

Beet Coleslaw 29

Jicama Coleslaw 30

Mediterranean Coleslaw 31

Bacon Turnip Coleslaw 32

Goat Cheese Grape Coleslaw 33

Vietnamese Coleslaw 34

Dijon Coleslaw 35

Chicago Coleslaw 36

Honey Mustard Coleslaw 37

Ham and Egg Coleslaw 38

Celery Root Coleslaw 39

Brussels Sprout Coleslaw 40

Cobb Coleslaw 41

Southwestern Coleslaw 42

Wasabi Snow Pea Coleslaw 43

Asparagus Coleslaw 44

Soy Ginger Coleslaw 45

Spicy Bok Choy Coleslaw 46

Ginger Ramen Coleslaw 47

Zucchini-Mozzarella Coleslaw 48

Green Papaya Peanut Coleslaw 49

Mango Peanut Coleslaw 50

Orange Fennel Coleslaw 51

Tri-Colored Coleslaw 52

Ginger Tahini Slaw 53

Carrots and Beets Coleslaw 55

Ranch Coleslaw 56

Sweet and Sour Coleslaw 57

Garden Coleslaw 58

Honey Mustard Coleslaw 59

Mango Lime Coleslaw 60

Texas Coleslaw 61

Raman Noodles Coleslaw 62

Memphis Style Coleslaw 63

Amish Coleslaw 64

German Coleslaw 65

Lexington Style North Carolina Red Coleslaw 66

Russian Coleslaw 67

Mexican Coleslaw 68

Asian Coleslaw 69

Hawaiian Coleslaw	70
Firecracker Coleslaw	71
Apple Bacon Coleslaw	72
Buttermilk Coleslaw	73
Sweet and Spicy Coleslaw	74
About the Author	75
Other Books by Laura Sommers	76
Cool Amazon Camping Merch	77

Introduction

Coleslaw is a dish that goes with many meals. During the summer, when outdoor cookouts happen almost every weekend, you know that coleslaw will be served.

Whether it is for a barbecue, family picnic, class reunion, pool party, deck party, cookout, get together or just as a side dish for one, there is nothing like a good heaping helping of coleslaw.

Coleslaw can be made many different ways with many different ingredients. There is a traditional coleslaw recipe, but there are also many regional and ethnic variations. This cookbook contains dozens of recipes that you have probably never imagined. So for your next party or meal, you can try any of these recipes to the surprise and delight of everyone, including yourself. Your coleslaw will never be boring again.

Classic Coleslaw

Ingredients:

3/4 cup mayonnaise
1/4 cup sour cream
3 tbsps. cider vinegar
1 tsp. sugar
1/2 tsp. kosher salt
1/2 head green cabbage, shredded
2 carrots, shredded

Directions:

1. Toss together cabbage and carrots in a large bowl.
2. In a separate smaller bowl, whisk together mayonnaise, sour cream, cider vinegar, sugar and kosher salt.
3. Pour mayonnaise mixture over the cabbage mixture.
4. Toss to coat.
5. Chill if desired.
6. Serve and enjoy!

Blue Cheese Herb Coleslaw

Ingredients:

3/4 cup mayonnaise
1/4 cup sour cream
3 tbsps. cider vinegar
1 tsp. sugar
1/2 tsp. kosher salt
1/2 head green cabbage, shredded
2 carrots, shredded
1 cup crumbled blue cheese
1/4 cup parsley, chopped
1/4 cup chives, chopped

Directions:

1. Toss together cabbage and carrots in a large bowl.
2. In a separate smaller bowl, whisk together mayonnaise, sour cream, cider vinegar, sugar and kosher salt.
3. Pour mayonnaise mixture over the cabbage mixture.
4. Toss to coat.
5. Add blue cheese, parsley and chives.
6. Toss again.
7. Chill if desired.
8. Serve and enjoy!

Buffalo Coleslaw

Ingredients:

3/4 cup mayonnaise
1/4 cup sour cream
3 tbsps. cider vinegar
1 tsp. sugar
1/2 tsp. kosher salt
1/2 head green cabbage, shredded
2 carrots, shredded
4 tbsps. buffalo hot sauce
1 cup celery, diced
1 cup crumbled blue cheese

Directions:

1. Toss together cabbage and carrots in a large bowl.
2. In a separate smaller bowl, whisk together mayonnaise, sour cream, cider vinegar, sugar and kosher salt.
3. Pour mayonnaise mixture over the cabbage mixture.
4. Toss to coat.
5. Add Buffalo sauce, celery and blue cheese.
6. Toss again.
7. Chill if desired.
8. Serve and enjoy!

Curry Coleslaw

Ingredients:

3/4 cup mayonnaise
1/4 cup Greek yogurt
3 tbsps. cider vinegar
1 tsp. sugar
1/2 tsp. kosher salt
1/2 head green cabbage, shredded
2 carrots, shredded
1/4 cup mango chutney
1 tbsp. curry powder
1 red bell pepper, diced
1/2 cup raisins
1/4 cup cilantro, chopped

Directions:

1. Toss together cabbage and carrots in a large bowl.
2. In a separate smaller bowl, whisk together mayonnaise, chutney, curry powder, yogurt, cider vinegar, sugar and kosher salt.
3. Pour mayonnaise mixture over the cabbage mixture.
4. Toss to coat.
5. Add bell pepper, raisins and cilantro.
6. Toss again.
7. Chill if desired.
8. Serve and enjoy!

Russian Coleslaw

Ingredients:

3/4 cup mayonnaise
1/2 cup red onion, sliced
1/4 cup sweet chili sauce
3 tbsps. cider vinegar
1 tsp. sugar
1/2 tsp. kosher salt
1/2 head green cabbage, shredded
2 carrots, shredded
1/4 cup parsley, chopped
1/4 cup sweet pickle relish

Directions:

1. Soak red onion in cold water for 15 minutes, then drain.
2. Toss together cabbage and carrots in a large bowl.
3. In a separate smaller bowl, whisk together mayonnaise, sweet chili sauce, parsley, pickle relish, cider vinegar, sugar and kosher salt.
4. Pour mayonnaise mixture over the cabbage mixture.
5. Toss to coat.
6. Chill if desired.
7. Serve and enjoy!

Waldorf Coleslaw

Ingredients:

3/4 cup mayonnaise
1/4 cup sour cream
3 tbsps. cider vinegar
3/4 cup apple, chopped
3/4 cup celery, diced
1 tsp. sugar
1/2 tsp. kosher salt
1/2 head green cabbage, shredded
1/2 cup walnuts, toasted and chopped

Directions:

1. Toss together cabbage, apples and celery in a large bowl.
2. In a separate smaller bowl, whisk together mayonnaise, sour cream, cider vinegar, sugar and kosher salt.
3. Pour mayonnaise mixture over the cabbage mixture.
4. Toss to coat.
5. Add walnuts.
6. Toss again.
7. Chill if desired.
8. Serve and enjoy!

Kohlrabi Apple Coleslaw

Ingredients:

3/4 cup mayonnaise
1/4 cup sour cream
3 tbsps. cider vinegar
2 tsps. sugar
1/2 tsp. kosher salt
3 tbsps. horseradish
1 tbsp. grainy mustard
1/4 head green cabbage, shredded
2 kohlrabi, julienned
2 apples, julienned
1/4 cup chopped dill

Directions:

1. Toss together cabbage, kohlrabi, apples and dill in a large bowl.
2. In a separate smaller bowl, whisk together mayonnaise, horseradish, mustard, sour cream, cider vinegar, sugar and kosher salt.
3. Pour mayonnaise mixture over the cabbage mixture.
4. Toss to coat.
5. Chill if desired.
6. Serve and enjoy!

Grape Pecan Coleslaw

Ingredients:

3/4 cup mayonnaise
1/4 cup sour cream
3 tbsps. cider vinegar
1 tsp. sugar
1/2 tsp. kosher salt
1/2 head red cabbage, shredded
2 carrots, shredded
1 cup red grapes, halved
1/2 cup toasted pecans, chopped
1/4 cup chives, chopped

Directions:

1. Toss together cabbage, grapes, pecans, chives and carrots in a large bowl.
2. In a separate smaller bowl, whisk together mayonnaise, sour cream, cider vinegar, sugar and kosher salt.
3. Pour mayonnaise mixture over the cabbage mixture.
4. Toss to coat.
5. Chill if desired.
6. Serve and enjoy!

Barbecue Chicken Coleslaw

Ingredients:

3/4 cup mayonnaise
1/4 cup sour cream
3 tbsps. cider vinegar
1 tsp. sugar
1/2 tsp. kosher salt
1/2 head green cabbage, shredded
2 carrots, shredded
1/3 cup barbecue sauce
2 cups cooked chicken, shredded
2 scallions, chopped

Directions:

1. Toss together cabbage, chicken, scallions and carrots in a large bowl.
2. In a separate smaller bowl, whisk together mayonnaise, barbecue sauce, sour cream, cider vinegar, sugar and kosher salt.
3. Pour mayonnaise mixture over the cabbage mixture.
4. Toss to coat.
5. Chill if desired.
6. Serve and enjoy!

Cajun Coleslaw

Ingredients:

3/4 cup mayonnaise
1/4 cup sour cream
2 tbsps. Creole mustard
2 tsps. Cajun seasoning
3 tbsps. cider vinegar
1 tsp. sugar
1/2 tsp. kosher salt
1/2 head green cabbage, shredded
2 carrots, shredded
1 cup bell pepper, julienned
1 cup celery, julienned
2 scallions, chopped

Directions:

1. Toss together cabbage, celery, scallions and carrots in a large bowl.
2. In a separate smaller bowl, whisk together mayonnaise, mustard, Cajun seasoning, sour cream, cider vinegar, sugar and kosher salt.
3. Pour mayonnaise mixture over the cabbage mixture.
4. Toss to coat.
5. Chill if desired.
6. Serve and enjoy!

Chipotle Coleslaw

Ingredients:

3/4 cup mayonnaise
1/4 cup sour cream
3 tbsps. cider vinegar
1 tsp. sugar
1/2 tsp. kosher salt
1/2 head green cabbage, shredded
1/4 cup cilantro, chopped
1 cup scallions, diced
1 cup red bell pepper, diced
1 cup jicama, diced
2 tbsps. puréed chipotles in adobo

Directions:

1. Toss together cabbage, cilantro, scallions, bell pepper and jicama in a large bowl.
2. In a separate smaller bowl, whisk together mayonnaise, chipotles, sour cream, cider vinegar, sugar and kosher salt.
3. Pour mayonnaise mixture over the cabbage mixture.
4. Toss to coat.
5. Chill if desired.
6. Serve and enjoy!

Crispy Coleslaw

Ingredients:

3/4 cup mayonnaise
1/4 cup sour cream
3 tbsps. cider vinegar
1 tsp. sugar
1/2 tsp. kosher salt
1/2 head green cabbage, shredded
1 tbsp. kosher salt

Directions:

1. Toss cabbage with 1 tbsp. kosher salt in a colander.
2. Let it sit 4 hours, then rinse and dry well.
3. In a separate smaller bowl, whisk together mayonnaise, sour cream, cider vinegar, sugar and 1/2 tsp. kosher salt.
4. Pour mayonnaise mixture over the cabbage mixture.
5. Toss to coat.
6. Chill if desired.
7. Serve and enjoy!

Carrot Pineapple Coleslaw

Ingredients:

1/2 cup mayonnaise
1/2 cup sour cream
2 tbsps. lemon juice
2 tbsps. sugar
1 tsp. kosher salt
12 carrots, shredded
1 cup raisins
1 cup diced pineapple
1/4 cup chives, diced

Directions:

1. Toss together carrots, raisins, pineapple and chives in a large bowl.
2. Whisk mayonnaise. sour cream, lemon juice, sugar, and salt together in a medium bowl.
3. Pour over carrot mixture.
4. Toss to coat.
5. Chill if desired.
6. Serve and enjoy!

Kale Coleslaw

Ingredients:

1/4 cup lemon juice,
1 tbsp. dijon mustard
1 tbsp. sugar
1 tsp. kosher salt
1/3 cup olive oil
5 cups green cabbage, shredded
5 cups Tuscan kale, shredded
2 carrots, shredded
1/2 cup toasted sunflower seeds

Directions:

1. Toss together Add cabbage, kale, carrots and sunflower seeds in a large bowl.
2. Whisk together lemon juice, dijon mustard, sugar, kosher salt and olive oil in a medium bowl.
3. Pour over cabbage mixture.
4. Toss to coat.
5. Chill if desired.
6. Serve and enjoy!

Light Coleslaw

Ingredients:

1/2 cup low-fat mayonnaise
1/2 cup Greek yogurt
3 tbsps. milk
3 tbsps. cider vinegar
1 tbsp. dijon mustard
1 tsp. sugar
Salt to taste
1/2 head green cabbage, shredded
1 carrot, shredded
1/4 cup fresh dill, chopped

Directions:

1. In a large bowl, toss together cabbage, carrot and dill.
2. In a separate bowl, whisk together the mayonnaise and Greek yogurt, vinegar, milk, dijon mustard, sugar, and salt.
3. Pour over cabbage mixture.
4. Toss to coat.
5. Chill if desired.
6. Serve and enjoy!

Broccoli Ranch Coleslaw

Ingredients:

1/2 cup buttermilk
1/4 cup mayonnaise
1/4 cup sour cream
3 tbsps. cider vinegar
1 tbsp. sugar
1 tsp. kosher salt
2 (12 oz.) bags broccoli slaw
1/4 cup parsley, chopped
1/4 cup chives, chopped
1/4 cup dill, chopped

Directions:

1. In a large bowl, toss together broccoli slaw, parsley, chives and dill.
2. In a separate bowl, whisk together buttermilk, mayonnaise, sour cream, vinegar, sugar and salt.
3. Pour over broccoli slaw mixture.
4. Toss to coat.
5. Chill if desired.
6. Serve and enjoy!

Thai Coleslaw

Ingredients:

1/2 cup peanut butter
1/3 cup rice vinegar
Juice of 2 limes
1 tbsp. grated ginger
1 tbsp. soy sauce
1/4 head napa cabbage, shredded
8 carrots, shredded
1/2 cup cilantro, chopped
1/2 cup scallions, diced
1/2 cup peanuts, chopped

Directions:

1. In a large bowl, toss together cabbage, carrots, cilantro, scallions and peanuts.
2. Purée together peanut butter, vinegar, lime juice, ginger and soy sauce.
3. Pour over cabbage mixture.
4. Toss to coat.
5. Chill if desired.
6. Serve and enjoy!

Pepper Coleslaw

Ingredients:

1 red onion, thinly sliced
2 tbsps. cider vinegar
1 1/2 tsps. sugar
1/2 tsp. thyme, chopped
1/4 cup olive oil
1 poblano, thinly sliced
4 sliced assorted bell peppers
1/2 tsp. kosher salt
Pepper to taste

Directions:

1. Soak red onion in cold water for 15 minutes.
2. Drain.
3. Whisk together vinegar, sugar, thyme and olive oil.
4. In a large bowl, toss together poblano, bell peppers, the onion and kosher salt.
5. Pour vinegar mixture over poblano mixture.
6. Toss to coat.
7. Pepper to taste.
8. Chill if desired.
9. Serve and enjoy!

Hot Dressed Coleslaw

Ingredients:

1/2 head green cabbage, roughly chopped
3 carrots
1/4 cup cider vinegar
2/3 cup vegetable oil
2 tbsps. sugar
2 tsps. kosher salt
1 tsp. celery seed,
1 tsp. mustard powder

Directions:

1. Pulse cabbage and carrots in a food processor until finely chopped.
2. in a medium pot, boil cider vinegar, vegetable oil, sugar, salt, mustard powder and celery seed for one minute.
3. Pour the dressing over the vegetables.
4. Toss to combine.
5. Serve and enjoy!

Apple Fennel Coleslaw

Ingredients:

1/2 head Savoy cabbage, shredded
1 tbsp. kosher salt
1/4 cup vegetable oil
1/4 cup cider vinegar
1/4 cup walnut oil
2 1/2 tsps. sugar
1 1/2 tbsps. dijon mustard
1 fennel bulb, thinly sliced
1 apple, thinly sliced
3/4 cup chopped walnuts

Directions:

1. Toss cabbage and salt in a colander.
2. Let sit for one hour in the sink.
3. Rinse and dry well then put in a large bowl.
4. Add fennel, apple and walnuts.
5. Toss together to mix.
6. Whisk together vegetable oil, walnut oil, vinegar, sugar, mustard in a medium bowl.
7. Pour vegetable oil mixture over the cabbage.
8. Toss to combine.
9. Chill if desired.
10. Serve and enjoy!

Creamy Coleslaw

Ingredients:

1/2 head green cabbage, roughly chopped
3 carrots
1/4 cup cider vinegar
2/3 cup vegetable oil
2 tbsps. sugar
2 tsps. kosher salt
1 tsp. celery seed
1 tsp. mustard powder
1/2 cup mayonnaise

Directions:

1. Pulse cabbage and carrots in a food processor until finely chopped.
2. in a medium pot, boil cider vinegar, vegetable oil, sugar, salt, mustard powder and celery seed for one minute.
3. Let cider mixture cool.
4. Add mayonnaise to cider mixture.
5. Pour the dressing over the vegetables.
6. Toss to combine.
7. Chill if desired.
8. Serve and enjoy!

Green Goddess Coleslaw

Ingredients:

1/2 cup parsley
1/2 cup chives
1/3 cup buttermilk,
1/3 cup olive oil
1/3 cup mayonnaise
2 tbsps. tarragon
2 tbsps. lemon juice
2 anchovies
2 (12 oz.) bags broccoli slaw

Directions:

1. In a blender or food processor, purée parsley, chives, buttermilk, olive oil, mayonnaise, tarragon. lemon juice, and anchovies.
2. Put broccoli slaw in a large bowl and pour puree over top.
3. Toss to combine.
4. Chill if desired.
5. Serve and enjoy!

Korean Coleslaw

Ingredients:

1/2 cup kimchi
3 tbsps. vegetable oil
3 tbsps. rice vinegar
2 tbsps. soy sauce
4 tsps. sesame oil
2 tsps. sugar
1/4 head napa cabbage, shredded
3 Asian pears, julienned
1 cucumber, thinly sliced
1/2 cup kimchi, chopped
Sesame seeds to taste

Directions:

1. In a large bowl, toss together cabbage, pears, cucumber and 1/2 cup chopped kimchi.
2. In a blender or food processor, purée 1/2 cup kimchi, vegetable oil, rice vinegar, soy sauce, sesame oil and sugar.
3. Pour puree mixture over the cabbage mixture.
4. Toss to combine.
5. Chill if desired.
6. Serve and enjoy!

Caesar Coleslaw

Ingredients:

1/2 head shredded Savoy cabbage
1 tbsp. kosher salt
1/2 cup olive oil
1/4 cup lemon juice
4 anchovies
1/4 tsp. honey
Croutons

Directions:

1. Toss cabbage with kosher salt in a colander.
2. Let it sit 1 hour in the sink, then rinse and dry well.
3. Put in a large bowl.
4. Purée olive oil, lemon juice, anchovies and honey.
5. Pour over cabbage mixture.
6. Toss to combine.
7. Chill if desired.
8. Add some crumbled croutons.
9. Toss again.
10. Serve and enjoy!

Vinaigrette Coleslaw

Ingredients:

1/2 cup white wine vinegar
2/3 cup olive oil
1 tbsp. kosher salt
2 tbsps. sugar
1/2 head red cabbage, shredded
1/2 head green cabbage, shredded
4 shredded carrots

Directions:

1. In a large bowl, toss red and green cabbage together with carrots.
2. In a medium bowl, whisk together vinegar, olive oil, salt and sugar.
3. Pour over cabbage mixture.
4. Toss to combine.
5. Chill if desired.
6. Add some crumbled croutons.
7. Toss again.
8. Serve and enjoy!

Confetti Coleslaw

Ingredients:

1/2 cup white wine vinegar
2/3 cup olive oil
1 tbsp. kosher salt
2 tbsps. sugar
1/4 head green cabbage, shredded
1/4 head red cabbage, shredded
3 carrots, shredded
2 bell peppers, thinly sliced
1/2 cup parsley, chopped

Directions:

1. In a large bowl, toss together cabbage, carrots, bell peppers and parsley.
2. In a medium bowl, whisk together vinegar, olive oil, salt and sugar.
3. Pour over cabbage mixture.
4. Toss to combine.
5. Chill if desired.
6. Add some crumbled croutons.
7. Toss again.
8. Serve and enjoy!

Herb Coleslaw

Ingredients:

1/2 cup white wine vinegar
2/3 cup olive oil
1 tbsp. kosher salt
2 tbsps. sugar
1/2 head red cabbage, shredded
1/2 head green cabbage, shredded
4 shredded carrots
2 tbsps. parsley, diced
2 tbsps. dill, diced
2 tbsps. chives, diced
2 tbsps. tarragon, diced

Directions:

1. In a large bowl, toss together cabbage together with carrots, parsley, dill, chaves and tarragon.
2. In a medium bowl, whisk together vinegar, olive oil, salt and sugar.
3. Pour over cabbage mixture.
4. Toss to combine.
5. Chill if desired.
6. Add some crumbled croutons.
7. Toss again.
8. Serve and enjoy!

Beet Coleslaw

Ingredients:

1/3 cup balsamic vinegar
2 tsps. kosher salt
1 tsp. honey
1/2 cup olive oil
1/4 head red cabbage, shredded
4 cups raw beets, peeled and shredded
Pistachios, chopped

Directions:

1. In a large bowl, toss together cabbage and beets.
2. In a medium bowl, whisk together vinegar, salt, honey and olive oil.
3. Pour over cabbage mixture.
4. Toss to combine.
5. Top with chopped pistachios.
6. Serve and enjoy!

Jicama Coleslaw

Ingredients:

3 tbsps. lime juice
1 1/2 tsps. ancho chile powder
1/4 tsp. cayenne pepper
1/4 cup vegetable oil
1 large jicama, julienned
1 cup pineapple, diced
1/2 English cucumber, julienned
1/2 red onion, thinly sliced
1/4 cup cilantro, chopped

Directions:

1. In a large bowl, toss together jicama, pineapple, cucumber, onion and cilantro.
2. In a medium bowl, whisk together lime juice, ancho chile powder, cayenne pepper and vegetable oil.
3. Pour over cabbage mixture.
4. Toss to combine.
5. Chill if desired.
6. Serve and enjoy!

Mediterranean Coleslaw

Ingredients:

1/3 cup tahini
1/3 cup yogurt
3 tbsps. lemon juice
1 tsp. honey
1 garlic clove, minced
Few dashes of hot sauce
1/2 head red cabbage, shredded
2 shredded carrots
1 Persian cucumber, thinly sliced
1 red bell pepper, thinly sliced

Directions:

1. In a large bowl, toss together cabbage, carrots and cucumber and red bell pepper.
2. In a medium bowl, whisk together yogurt, tahini, lemon juice, honey, garlic and hot sauce.
3. Pour over cabbage mixture.
4. Toss to combine.
5. Chill if desired.
6. Serve and enjoy!

Bacon Turnip Coleslaw

Ingredients:

4 slices bacon
2 tbsps. vegetable oil
2 tbsps. cider vinegar
2 tbsps. grainy mustard
1 tsp. celery seeds
1/3 cup sour cream
6 cups julienned turnips
3 cups shredded green cabbage
1/4 cup chopped parsley

Directions:

1. Cook bacon until crisp.
2. Reserve 2 tbsps. of the bacon drippings.
3. Drain bacon on paper towels and then crumble.
4. In a medium bowl, whisk together bacon drippings, vegetable oil, cider vinegar and mustard.
5. Whisk in celery seeds and sour cream.
6. In a large bowl, toss together turnips, cabbage, parsley and crumbled bacon.
7. Pour oil and vinegar mixture over the cabbage mixture.
8. Toss to combine.
9. Chill if desired.
10. Serve and enjoy!

Goat Cheese Grape Coleslaw

Ingredients:

1/2 cup olive oil
2 tbsps. dijon mustard
2 tbsps. honey
2 tbsps. white wine vinegar
1/2 tsp. kosher salt
1/2 head napa cabbage, roughly chopped
1/2 cup grapes
1/4 cup goat cheese, crumbled
1/4 cup toasted hazelnuts, chopped
Chives, chopped

Directions:

1. In a large bowl, toss together cabbage, grapes, goat cheese and hazelnuts.
2. In a medium bowl, whisk together olive oil, mustard, honey, vinegar and salt.
3. Pour over cabbage mixture.
4. Toss to combine.
5. Sprinkle with chopped chives.
6. Serve and enjoy!

Vietnamese Coleslaw

Ingredients:

1/3 cup white vinegar
2 1/2 tbsps. sugar
1/3 cup vegetable oil
3 cups carrots, julienned
3 cups daikon, julienned
2 cups English cucumber, julienned
1 jalapeño, diced
1/4 cup cilantro, chopped
1/4 cup mint, chopped

Directions:

1. In a large bowl, toss together daikon, carrots, cucumber, jalapeño, mint and cilantro.
2. In a medium bowl, whisk together vinegar, sugar and vegetable oil.
3. Pour over cabbage mixture.
4. Toss to combine.
5. Chill if desired.
6. Serve and enjoy!

Dijon Coleslaw

Ingredients:

1/4 cup cider vinegar
2 tbsps. dijon mustard
1 tbsp. sugar
1 tbsp. kosher salt
2/3 cup olive oil
1/2 head green cabbage, shredded
1/4 head red cabbage, shredded
2 carrots, shredded
2 scallions, diced

Directions:

1. In a large bowl, toss together cabbage, carrots and scallions.
2. In a medium bowl, whisk together vinegar, mustard, sugar, salt and olive oil.
3. Pour over cabbage mixture.
4. Toss to combine.
5. Chill if desired.
6. Serve and enjoy!

Chicago Coleslaw

Ingredients:

1/4 cup cider vinegar
2 tbsps. yellow mustard
1 tbsp. sugar
1 tbsp. kosher salt
2/3 cup olive oil
1/2 head shredded green cabbage,
2 shredded carrots,
1/2 cup sweet pickle relish
1/2 cup pickled sport peppers, chopped
2 tsps. celery seeds

Directions:

1. In a large bowl, toss together cabbage, carrots, pickle relish and peppers.
2. In a medium bowl, whisk together vinegar, mustard, sugar, salt, olive oil and celery seeds.
3. Pour over cabbage mixture.
4. Toss to combine.
5. Chill if desired.
6. Serve and enjoy!

Honey Mustard Coleslaw

Ingredients:

1/4 cup cider vinegar
2 tbsps. honey mustard
1 tbsp. kosher salt
2/3 cup olive oil
1/2 head green cabbage, shredded
1/4 head red cabbage, shredded
2 carrots, shredded
2 scallions, diced
2 julienned apples
1/2 cup toasted sliced almonds
Honey to taste

Directions:

1. In a large bowl, toss together cabbage, carrots, scallions, apples and almonds.
2. In a medium bowl, whisk together vinegar, mustard, salt, honey and olive oil.
3. Pour over cabbage mixture.
4. Toss to combine.
5. Chill if desired.
6. Serve and enjoy!

Ham and Egg Coleslaw

Ingredients:

1/4 cup cider vinegar
2 tbsps. dijon mustard
1 tbsp. sugar
1 tbsp. kosher salt
2/3 cup olive oil
1/2 head green cabbage, shredded
1/4 head red cabbage, shredded
2 carrots, shredded
2 scallions, diced
1/4 pound diced ham
2 hard boiled eggs, chopped

Directions:

1. In a large bowl, toss together cabbage, carrots and scallions.
2. In a medium bowl, whisk together vinegar, mustard, sugar, salt and olive oil.
3. Pour over cabbage mixture.
4. Toss to combine.
5. add ham and eggs.
6. Toss again.
7. Chill if desired.
8. Serve and enjoy!

Celery Root Coleslaw

Ingredients:

3/4 cup mayonnaise
1/4 cup sour cream
Juice of 2 lemons
2 tbsps. dijon mustard
1 tsp. sugar
1/2 tsp. kosher salt
1/4 head green cabbage, shredded
4 cups celery root, shredded
1/4 cup parsley, chopped

Directions:

1. In a large bowl, toss together cabbage, celery root and parsley.
2. In a medium bowl, whisk together mayonnaise, sour cream, lemon juice, mustard, sugar and salt.
3. Pour over cabbage mixture.
4. Toss to combine.
5. Chill if desired.
6. Serve and enjoy!

Brussels Sprout Coleslaw

Ingredients:

4 slices bacon
2 tbsps. olive oil
2 tbsps. maple syrup
1/3 cup sherry vinegar
6 cups shredded Brussels sprouts
1 shallot, thinly sliced
Salt and pepper to taste

Directions:

1. Cook bacon until crisp.
2. Reserve 2 tbsps. of the bacon drippings.
3. Drain bacon on paper towels and then crumble.
4. In a large bowl, toss together Brussels sprouts, shallot and bacon.
5. In a medium bowl, whisk together bacon drippings, olive oil, maple syrup and sherry vinegar.
6. Pour over cabbage mixture.
7. Toss to combine.
8. Salt and pepper to taste.
9. Serve and enjoy!

Cobb Coleslaw

Ingredients:

1 avocado, peeled and deseeded
1/3 cup lemon juice
1/3 cup olive oil
1/3 cup water
1/2 tsp. kosher salt
1/2 large head green cabbage, shredded
1 cup diced tomato
1 cup crumbled blue cheese
3 hard boiled eggs, chopped
1/2 cup crumbled cooked bacon

Directions:

1. In a large bowl, toss together cabbage, tomato, blue cheese, and eggs.
2. Purée together avocado, lemon juice, olive oil, water, and salt.
3. Pour over cabbage mixture.
4. Toss to combine.
5. Top with crumbled bacon.
6. Serve and enjoy!

Southwestern Coleslaw

Ingredients:

1 avocado, peeled and deseeded
1/3 cup lemon juice
1/3 cup olive oil
1/3 cup water
1/2 tsp. kosher salt
3 cups red cabbage, shredded
3 cups green cabbage, shredded
1 tbsp. kosher salt
1 cup corn
1 poblano, thinly sliced
1 small bunch scallions, chopped

Directions:

1. Toss together cabbage and salt in a large colander.
2. Let it sit 1 hour in the sink.
3. Rinse and dry well.
4. Purée together avocado, lemon juice, olive oil, water, and salt.
5. Pour over cabbage mixture.
6. Toss to combine.
7. Add corn, poblano and scallions.
8. Toss again.
9. Serve and enjoy!

Wasabi Snow Pea Coleslaw

Ingredients:

1 cup mayonnaise
2 tsps. rice vinegar
2 tsps. wasabi paste
1 tsp. sugar
1 tsp. kosher salt
1/2 head napa cabbage, shredded
2 cups snow peas, thinly sliced
2 tsps. sesame seeds

Directions:

1. In a large bowl, toss together cabbage and snow peas.
2. In a medium bowl, whisk together mayonnaise, wasabi paste, vinegar, sugar, salt and sesame seeds
3. Pour over cabbage mixture.
4. Toss to combine.
5. Serve and enjoy!

Asparagus Coleslaw

Ingredients:

1/4 cup lemon juice
1 tbsp. dijon mustard
2 tsps. sugar
1/2 cup olive oil
1/2 head shredded napa cabbage
1 pound asparagus, thinly sliced
2 shallots, thinly sliced
1 cup shaved Parmesan

Directions:

1. In a large bowl, toss together cabbage, asparagus, shallots and Parmesan.
2. In a medium bowl, whisk together lemon juice, dijon mustard, sugar and olive oil.
3. Pour over cabbage mixture.
4. Toss to combine.
5. Chill if desired.
6. Serve and enjoy!

Soy Ginger Coleslaw

Ingredients:

1/3 cup rice vinegar
3 tbsps. soy sauce
3 tbsps. orange juice
1 tbsp. sugar
1 tbsp. grated ginger
1 tsp. sesame oil
1/2 cup vegetable oil
1/2 head napa cabbage, shredded
2 carrots, shredded
1 cup snow peas, thinly sliced
2 Fresno chiles, thinly sliced

Directions:

1. In a large bowl, toss together cabbage, carrots, snow peas and chiles.
2. In a medium bowl, whisk together vinegar, soy sauce, orange juice, sugar, ginger, sesame oil and vegetable oil.
3. Pour over cabbage mixture.
4. Toss to combine.
5. Chill if desired.
6. Serve and enjoy!

Spicy Bok Choy Coleslaw

Ingredients:

1/3 cup rice vinegar
3 tbsps. soy sauce
3 tbsps. orange juice
1 tbsp. sugar
1 tbsp. grated ginger
1 tsp. sesame oil
1/2 cup vegetable oil
9 cups bok choy, thinly sliced
2 carrots, shredded
1 cup snow peas, thinly sliced
2 Fresno chiles, thinly sliced
2 tbsps. Sriracha

Directions:

1. In a large bowl, toss together bok choy, carrots, snow peas and chiles.
2. In a medium bowl, whisk together vinegar, soy sauce, Sriracha, orange juice, sugar, ginger, sesame oil and vegetable oil.
3. Pour over cabbage mixture.
4. Toss to combine.
5. Chill if desired.
6. Serve and enjoy!

Ginger Ramen Coleslaw

Ingredients:

1/3 cup rice vinegar
3 tbsps. soy sauce
3 tbsps. orange juice
1 tbsp. sugar
1 tbsp. grated ginger
1 tsp. sesame oil
1/2 cup vegetable oil
1/2 head napa cabbage, shredded
1 cup snow peas, thinly sliced
2 carrots, shredded
2 red bell peppers, thinly sliced
2 cups raw ramen noodles, crumbled
1/4 cup scallions, roughly chopped

Directions:

1. In a large bowl, toss together cabbage, carrots, bell peppers, ramen noodles, scallions and snow peas.
2. In a medium bowl, whisk together vinegar, soy sauce, orange juice, sugar, ginger, sesame oil and vegetable oil.
3. Pour over cabbage mixture.
4. Toss to combine.
5. Chill if desired.
6. Serve and enjoy!

Zucchini-Mozzarella Coleslaw

Ingredients:

1/4 cup red wine vinegar
1 tbsp. dijon mustard
1 tsp. kosher salt
1/3 cup olive oil
3 shredded zucchini
1 cup julienned tomato
1 cup fresh mozzarella
1/2 cup basil, shredded
Pine nuts, toasted

Directions:

1. In a large bowl, toss together zucchini, tomato, mozzarella and basil.
2. In a medium bowl, whisk together vinegar, mustard, salt and olive oil.
3. Pour over zucchini mixture.
4. Toss to combine.
5. Chill if desired.
6. Top with toasted pine nuts.
7. Serve and enjoy!

Green Papaya Peanut Coleslaw

Ingredients:

3 tbsps. fish sauce
1/4 cup lime juice
1/4 cup vegetable oil
1 tsp. kosher salt
2 sliced Thai bird chiles
6 cups green papaya, julienned
1 large red bell pepper, julienned
1/2 cup cilantro, chopped
1/2 cup peanuts, chopped

Directions:

1. In a large bowl, toss together papaya, bell pepper, cilantro and peanuts.
2. In a medium bowl, whisk together fish sauce, lime juice, vegetable oil, salt and chiles.
3. Pour over papaya mixture.
4. Toss to combine.
5. Chill if desired.
6. Top with toasted pine nuts.
7. Serve and enjoy!

Mango Peanut Coleslaw

Ingredients:

3 tbsps. fish sauce
1/4 cup lime juice
1/4 cup vegetable oil
2 sliced Thai bird chiles
6 cups firm mango, julienned
1 large red bell pepper, julienned
1/2 cup cilantro, chopped
1/2 cup peanuts, chopped

Directions:

1. In a large bowl, toss together mango, bell pepper, cilantro and peanuts.
2. In a medium bowl, whisk together fish sauce, lime juice, vegetable oil and chiles.
3. Pour over papaya mixture.
4. Toss to combine.
5. Chill if desired.
6. Top with toasted pine nuts.
7. Serve and enjoy!

Orange Fennel Coleslaw

Ingredients:

1 cup red onion, thinly sliced
1/4 cup champagne vinegar
2 tbsps. grainy mustard
1 tbsp. kosher salt
1 1/2 tsps. sugar
2/3 cup olive oil
5 cups fennel, julienned
5 cups green cabbage, julienned
2 oranges, pealed and segmented

Directions:

1. Soak the onion slices in cold water for 15 minutes then drain.
2. In a large bowl, toss together the fennel and cabbage.
3. In a medium bowl, whisk together vinegar, mustard, salt, sugar and olive oil.
4. Pour over the cabbage mixture.
5. Toss to combine.
6. Add the red onion and oranges.
7. Toss again.
8. Serve and enjoy!

Tri-Colored Coleslaw

Ingredients:

1/2 head green cabbage, cored
1/2 head red cabbage, cored
1 pound carrots, peeled and shredded
1 large bunch cilantro, leaves roughly chopped
3 limes, juiced (about 1/3 cup)
2/3 cup neutral oil, such as peanut or safflower
1 to 2 tsp. sugar
Kosher salt and freshly ground pepper

Directions:

1. Shred the cabbage finely in using a chef's knife, a mandoline, or a food processor's shredding blad.
2. In a very large bowl, toss together the shredded cabbage with the shredded carrots and chopped cilantro.
3. Whisk the lime juice and oil together in a bowl or measuring cup, and whisk in the sugar.
4. Toss with the slaw, and season generously with salt and pepper (it may need more than you think it will at first, and this salad definitely needs its salt!).
5. Best served within a day or two, cold from the fridge, but you can refrigerate it for up to 3 days or until it loses its crispness.

Ginger Tahini Slaw

Dressing Ingredients:

3 scallions, white and light green parts only, minced
1/4 cup low sodium tamari or soy sauce
1/4 cup water
2 tbsps. tahini
1 tbsp. fresh lime juice
1 tbsp. rice wine vinegar
1 tbsp. pure maple syrup
1 1/2 tbsp. freshly grated ginger
1/2 tsp. crushed red pepper flakes

Salad Ingredients:

2 cups shredded red cabbage
1/2 cup shredded napa cabbage
2 carrots, coarsely grated
1 medium-sized beet, coarsely grated
1 cup cilantro, finely chopped
1 jalapeño pepper, seeded and cut into thin slivers
1 cup cooked, shelled edamame
1/2 cup peanuts
1/2 cup raisins
2 tbsps. sesame seeds

Directions:

1. Prepare the dressing by whisking all of the ingredients together until smooth and well-combined. This works best with an immersion blender but a hand whisk is fine too. Taste the dressing and adjust seasonings if needed.
2. Place the red cabbage, Napa cabbage, carrots, beets, edamame, cilantro and jalapeño in a large bowl.
3. Stir to combine.
4. Pour the dressing over the cabbage mixture and toss until everything is evenly coated.
5. Add the peanuts, raisins, and sesame seeds.

6. Serve chilled or at room temperature.

Carrots and Beets Coleslaw

Ingredients:

Zest and juice of 1 orange (about 1 tbsp. zest, 1/2 cup juice)
1 tsp. cumin seeds, toasted
3 tbsps. sherry vinegar
1 tbsp. extra virgin olive oil
1/2 tsp. sugar
3 medium carrots (about 8 oz.)
2 medium beets (about 8 oz.)
1 small celery root (about 10 oz.)
Salt and freshly ground pepper

Directions:

1. In a large bowl, whisk together the orange zest and juice, cumin seeds, vinegar, olive oil, and sugar.
2. Peel and shred the carrots, beets, and celery root and add to the bowl.
3. Toss to combine.
4. Season to taste with salt and pepper.
5. For best flavor, refrigerate for at least 30 minutes before serving.

Ranch Coleslaw

Salad Ingredients:

3 cups coleslaw mix
1/4 cup Mexicorn, drained
1 jalapeno pepper, seeded and chopped
2 tbs chopped red onion
1 tbs cilantro
1/2 cup shredded cheddar cheese

Dressing Ingredients:

1/2 cup ranch dressing
1 1/2 tsp lime juice
1/2 tsp cumin

Directions:

1. Mix together all of the salad ingredients in a large bowl.
2. In a small bowl, whisk the salad dressing, lime juice, and Red Monkey cumin.
3. Pour this mixture over the coleslaw, and toss to coat.
4. Refrigerate until you are ready to serve.

Sweet and Sour Coleslaw

Ingredients:

1/2 medium head green cabbage, finely shredded (4 cups)
1 large carrot, finely shredded (1 cup)
1 medium green bell pepper, chopped (1 cup)
4 medium green onions, thinly sliced (1/4 cup)
1/2 cup sugar
1/2 cup white wine vinegar, white vinegar or cider vinegar
1/4 cup vegetable oil
1 tsp. ground mustard
1/2 tsp. celery seed
1/2 tsp. salt

Directions:

1. In large glass or plastic bowl, place cabbage, carrot, bell pepper and onions.
2. In tightly covered container, shake remaining ingredients.
3. Pour over vegetables.
4. Stir.
5. Cover and refrigerate at least 3 hours, stirring several times, until chilled and flavors are blended.
6. Stir before serving; serve with slotted spoon.

Garden Coleslaw

Ingredients:

7 cups coleslaw mix
1 small zucchini, shredded (about 1 cup)
1 cup shredded carrots (1 1/2 medium)
1/2 cup finely chopped green bell pepper (1/2 medium)
3/4 cup mayonnaise or salad dressing
2 tbsps. sugar
2 tsps. lemon juice
1 tsp. celery seed
1/2 tsp. salt

Directions:

1. In large bowl, gently mix ingredients.
2. Refrigerate 15 to 20 minutes before serving.

Honey Mustard Coleslaw

Dressing Ingredients:

2 (6 oz. each) containers lemon yogurt
1/4 cup honey mustard
1 1/2 tsps. seasoned salt
4 tsps. lemon juice
2 tsps. grated lemon peel

Salad Ingredients:

1 bag (16 oz) coleslaw mix (8 cups)
1 small zucchini, shredded (about 1 cup)
1 cup shredded carrots
1/2 medium cucumber, quartered lengthwise, cut into 1/4-inch slices (1 cup)
1/2 cup chopped red bell pepper
4 strips bacon, cooked, chopped

Directions:

1. In medium bowl, mix dressing ingredients until well blended and smooth.
2. In large bowl, mix all salad ingredients except bacon.
3. Add dressing; toss to mix well.
4. Serve immediately or refrigerate until serving time. Spoon into serving bowl; sprinkle with bacon.

Mango Lime Coleslaw

Ingredients:

2 containers (6 oz each) Yoplait® Original yogurt Key lime pie
1 tbsp. sugar
2 tbsps. vinegar
1/2 tsp. ground cumin
5 cups coleslaw blend (from 16-oz bag)
1 large mango, seed removed, peeled and chopped (about 1 1/2 cups)

Directions:

1. In small bowl, mix yogurt, sugar, vinegar and cumin.
2. In 2-quart serving bowl, place coleslaw blend.
3. Top with mango; spoon yogurt mixture over mango.
4. Serve immediately, or cover tightly and refrigerate up to 8 hours. Before serving, toss salad lightly to mix.

Texas Coleslaw

Ingredients:

1 (16 oz.) package coleslaw mix
1 (7 oz.) can Mexican-style corn, drained
1 cup shredded Cheddar cheese
2 fresh jalapeno peppers, seeded and chopped
1/2 cup chopped fresh cilantro
1 cup creamy ranch salad dressing
1/4 tsp. ground cumin 1/4 tsp. ground coriander
1/2 tsp. garlic powder
1 lime, juiced

Directions:

1. In a large bowl, toss together the coleslaw mix, corn, Cheddar cheese, jalapeno and cilantro.
2. In a separate bowl, stir together the Ranch-style dressing, cumin, coriander, garlic powder and lime juice.
3. Pour over the coleslaw mixture, and toss to coat.
4. Refrigerate until serving.

Raman Noodles Coleslaw

Ingredients:

2 tbsp. vegetable oil
3 tbsp. white wine vinegar
2 tbsp. white sugar
1 pkg. chicken flavored ramen noodles, crushed, seasoning packet reserved
1/2 tsp. salt
1/2 tsp. ground black pepper
2 tbsp. sesame seeds
1/4 cup sliced almonds
1/2 med. head cabbage, shredded
5 green onions, chopped

Directions:

1. Preheat oven to 350 degrees F.
2. In a medium bowl, whisk together the oil, vinegar, sugar, ramen noodle spice mix, salt and pepper to create a dressing.
3. Place sesame seeds and almonds in a single layer on a medium baking sheet.
4. Bake in the preheated oven 10 minutes, or until lightly brown.
5. In a large salad bowl, combine the cabbage, green onions and crushed ramen noodles.
6. Pour dressing over the cabbage, and toss to coat evenly.
7. Top with toasted sesame seeds and almonds.

Memphis Style Coleslaw

Ingredients:

1 cup mayonnaise
2 tbsp. dijon mustard
2 tbsp. apple cider vinegar
3 tsps. sugar
3/4 tsp. kosher salt
1 tsp. onion powder or 1 tbsp. finely grated onion
2 tsps. celery seeds
1 16 oz. bag of coleslaw mix

Directions:

1. In a large bowl, stir together the mayonnaise, mustard, vinegar, sugar, salt, onion powder, and celery seeds.
2. Add the shredded cabbage and toss until well coated.
3. Refrigerate for at least an hour before serving.
4. Toss again right before serving.
5. Serve and enjoy!

Amish Coleslaw

Ingredients:

1 head of cabbage
2 carrots
1 pepper
1/2 cup vinegar
Pepper & salt
1 stalk celery
1 onion
1 cup sugar
1/2 tsp. celery salt

Directions:

1. Chop cabbage, onion, celery, carrots and pepper.
2. Squeeze out moisture.
3. Salt and set aside.
4. Combine sugar, vinegar, celery salt, salt and pepper.
5. Bring to a boil.

German Coleslaw

Ingredients:

/2 head cabbage, thinly sliced
3 tbsps. white sugar
3 tbsps. cider vinegar
1/2 tsp. celery seed
1/2 tsp. salt
1/2 cup mayonnaise, or more to taste

Directions:

1. Place cabbage in a large bowl.
2. Mix sugar, vinegar, celery seed, and salt together in a separate bowl.
3. Stir mayonnaise into sugar-vinegar mixture until dressing is smooth and creamy.
4. Pour dressing over cabbage; toss to coat.
5. Marinate coleslaw in refrigerator for 2 to 3 hours; stir well before serving.
6. Add to cabbage mixture and refrigerate.

Lexington Style North Carolina Red Coleslaw

4 cups finely shredded cabbage
1/3 cup apple cider vinegar
1/3 cup ketchup
2 tbsps. white sugar
2 tsps. crushed red pepper flakes, or to taste
2 dashes hot pepper sauce, or to taste

Directions:

1. Place the cabbage into a salad bowl.
2. In a small bowl, whisk together apple cider vinegar, ketchup, sugar, red pepper flakes, and hot sauce until the sugar has dissolved.

Russian Coleslaw

Ingredients:

1 lg. cabbage, grated
1/2 bell pepper, grated
1 lg. onion, grated
1/2 cup oil
1 tsp. dry mustard
1/2 cup sugar
1/2 cup white vinegar
1 tsp. salt
1 tsp. celery seed

Directions:

1. Combine cabbage, bell pepper, and onion.
2. Combine oil, sugar, vinegar, salt, dry mustard and celery seed; boil this mixture for 1 minute.
3. Pour oil mixture over cabbage mixture and mix well.
4. Set in refrigerator overnight or at least 4 hours. Slaw stays good at least 1 week.
5. Pour the dressing over the cabbage, toss thoroughly, and refrigerate at least 1 hour before serving.

Mexican Coleslaw

Ingredients:

1 head of cabbage, shredded
2 tbsp. salt
2 lrg. onions, chopped fine
1 lrg. bell pepper
1 cup sugar
1 1/2 cup white vinegar
tsp. celery seed
2 small hot peppers

Directions:

1. Shred all together.
2. Add sugar and vinegar.
3. Chill before serving.
4. Serve and enjoy!

Asian Coleslaw

Ingredients:

6 tbsps. rice wine vinegar
6 tbsps. vegetable oil
5 tbsps. creamy peanut butter
3 tbsps. soy sauce
3 tbsps. brown sugar
2 tbsps. minced fresh ginger root
1 1/2 tbsps. minced garlic
5 cups thinly sliced green cabbage
2 cups thinly sliced red cabbage
2 cups shredded napa cabbage
2 red bell peppers, thinly sliced
2 carrots, julienned
6 green onions, chopped
1/2 cup chopped fresh cilantro

Directions:

1. In a medium bowl, whisk together the rice vinegar, oil, peanut butter, soy sauce, brown sugar, ginger, and garlic.
2. In a large bowl, mix the green cabbage, red cabbage, napa cabbage, red bell peppers, carrots, green onions, and cilantro.
3. Toss with the peanut butter mixture just before serving.
4. Serve and enjoy!

Hawaiian Coleslaw

Ingredients:

1 (14 oz.) bag coleslaw mix
1 1/4 cups mayonnaise
1 (8 oz.) can crushed pineapple, drained
1 (6 oz.) can Mandarin oranges, drained
1/4 cup chopped Maraschino cherries
1/4 tsp. salt
1/4 tsp. black pepper

Directions:

1. In a large bowl, toss together all ingredients until well mixed and evenly coated.
2. Cover and chill for 1 to 2 hours.
3. Mix again before serving.
4. Serve and enjoy!

Firecracker Coleslaw

Ingredients:

1 (16 oz.) package shredded coleslaw mix
3 stalks celery, chopped
1/2 red bell pepper, chopped
1/2 yellow bell pepper, chopped
1 jalapeno pepper, finely diced, seeds removed
1 cup Italian dressing
2 tbsp. light brown sugar

Directions:

1. In a large bowl, combine the coleslaw mix, celery, and red and yellow bell peppers.
2. In a small bowl, whisk together the Italian dressing and the brown sugar until the sugar dissolves; pour over the cabbage mixture, tossing to coat completely.
3. Cover, and chill for at least 1 hour before serving.
4. Serve and enjoy!

Apple Bacon Coleslaw

Ingredients:

3 tbsps. olive oil
2 tbsps. mayonnaise
1 tbsp. Dijon mustard
1 tbsp. lemon juice
1/2 tbsp. hot sauce
1 tbsp. sugar
1/4 tsp. salt
1 (16 oz.) package shredded coleslaw mix
1 large apple, diced
4 slices cooked bacon, crumbled

Directions:

1. In a large bowl, whisk together olive oil, mayonnaise, mustard, lemon juice, hot sauce, sugar, and salt.
2. Add coleslaw mix and apple, and toss until evenly coated.
3. Sprinkle with bacon and serve, or cover and refrigerate until ready to serve.

Buttermilk Coleslaw

Ingredients:

2 (16 oz.) packages shredded coleslaw mix
2 cups mayonnaise
1 cup buttermilk
3 tbsp. white sugar
1 tsp. celery seed
1/2 tsp. ground black pepper

Directions:

1. In a large bowl, stir together the mayonnaise, buttermilk, sugar, celery seed and black pepper.
2. Fold in the coleslaw mix, and refrigerate until serving.
3. Chill for at least an hour before serving.
4. Serve and enjoy!

Sweet and Spicy Coleslaw

Ingredients:

1 small green cabbage
4 carrots
1 med. onion
1/2 cup mayonnaise
1/4 cup mustard
2 tsp. apple cider vinegar
1 cup sugar
Freshly ground black pepper
1/2 tsp. cayenne pepper
Kosher salt

Directions:

1. Chop the cabbage in to fine shreds.
2. Peel and chop the carrots julienned.
3. Peel and chop the onion.
4. Toss the chopped vegetables in a large bowl.
5. Whisk together in a separate bowl the mayonnaise, mustard, cider vinegar, sugar, 1 tsp. black pepper and the cayenne in a medium bowl.
6. Toss the dressing with the cabbage mixture.
7. Season with salt and pepper.
8. Cover with plastic wrap and chill at least 2 hours before serving.
9. Serve and enjoy!

About the Author

Laura Sommers is The Recipe Lady!

She lives on a small farm in Baltimore County, Maryland and has a passion for food. She has taken cooking classes in Memphis, New Orleans and Washington DC. She has been a taste tester for a large spice company in Baltimore and written food reviews for several local papers. She loves writing cookbooks with the most delicious recipes to share her knowledge and love of cooking with the world.

Follow her on Pinterest:

http://pinterest.com/therecipelady1

Visit the Recipe Lady's blog for even more great recipes.

http://the-recipe-lady.blogspot.com/

Visit her Amazon Author Page to see her latest books:

amazon.com/author/laurasommers

Follow the Recipe Lady on Facebook:

https://www.facebook.com/therecipegirl

Follow her on Twitter:

https://twitter.com/TheRecipeLady1

Other Books by Laura Sommers

- Egg Salad Recipes
- Deviled Egg Recipes
- Corn on the Cob Cookbook
- Potato Salad Recipes
- Hamburger Recipes
- Salsa Recipes
- Pasta Salad Recipes
- Green Peas Recipes
- Frittata Recipes
- Stuffed Baked Potato Cookbook
- Pot Pie Recipes
- Chip Dip Cookbook
- Hot Dog Cookbook

Printed in Great Britain
by Amazon